W9-CRS-000

OFF-ROAD VEHICLES

Have an adult help you remove the perforated sticker pages.

Off-Road Facts

Off-road vehicles are very fast and powerful. They move easily across difficult obstacles like rocks, mud, and sand.

Off-road races can run hundreds of miles across the sweltering desert.

Dune buggies are equipped with roll cages to protect drivers when they flip.

Huge monster trucks can crush a whole row of cars!

Off-roaders can ride on rocky, muddy, steep, and soft ground with ultra-gripping chunky tires.

Snowmobiles use skis up front to race over icy surfaces in winter.

Dirt and mud are no match
for this powerful pick-up!

A hovercraft has fans that create
a cushion of pressurized air for
gliding above land or water.

Rally cars are sent on a twisting
course through woods, jumps, and
awesome water crossings.

A motocross can easily maneuver
on loose ground and leap over
massive dirt mounds.

Rock-crawlers can tilt on an
angle when drivers want to
scale huge rocks!

Did You Know That?

Off-road racing is a very popular sport! Daredevil teams travel long distances across all kinds of terrain to compete for the top prize.

Monster trucks have wheels that are as tall as a grown adult!

Amphibian vehicles are made for driving on land or through water.

At the beginning of a race, the racers line up at the starting line.

Quad bikes take drivers through hills, deep puddles, open fields, and woodland tracks.

Rally cars have a co-driver who calls out what's up ahead on the road.

Some trucks were created and used by the military.

Many off-road vehicles are equipped with fog lights and extra road lamps.

Trucks compete alongside 4x4s and motorbikes in the renowned Paris-Dakar desert rally.

Sidecar motocross bikes rely on passengers to move their bodies to go faster in turns and jumps.

Thick tire treads help off-road vehicles grip difficult surfaces.

Drivers wear harnesses to protect against high-impact skids, flips, and tumbles.

Stadium Showdown

These monstrous off-road vehicles are showing off their power in the crowded stadium. Use your stickers to bring this scene to life.

16

2–3

6–11

14–15

12-13

4-5

6-11

All-Terrain Vehicles

Any weather is perfect for a wild race, but not every vehicle is equipped for all seasons. Place each machine over the shadow that matches its terrain.

Sand dunes

Jungle

Mud

Canyons

Desert

Swamp

Forest

Snow

Color Crazy!

The race is on! Help these off-roaders make it to the finish line by matching up their colors with each racing flag.

Can You Spot...

Guess which sticker matches each of these shadows.

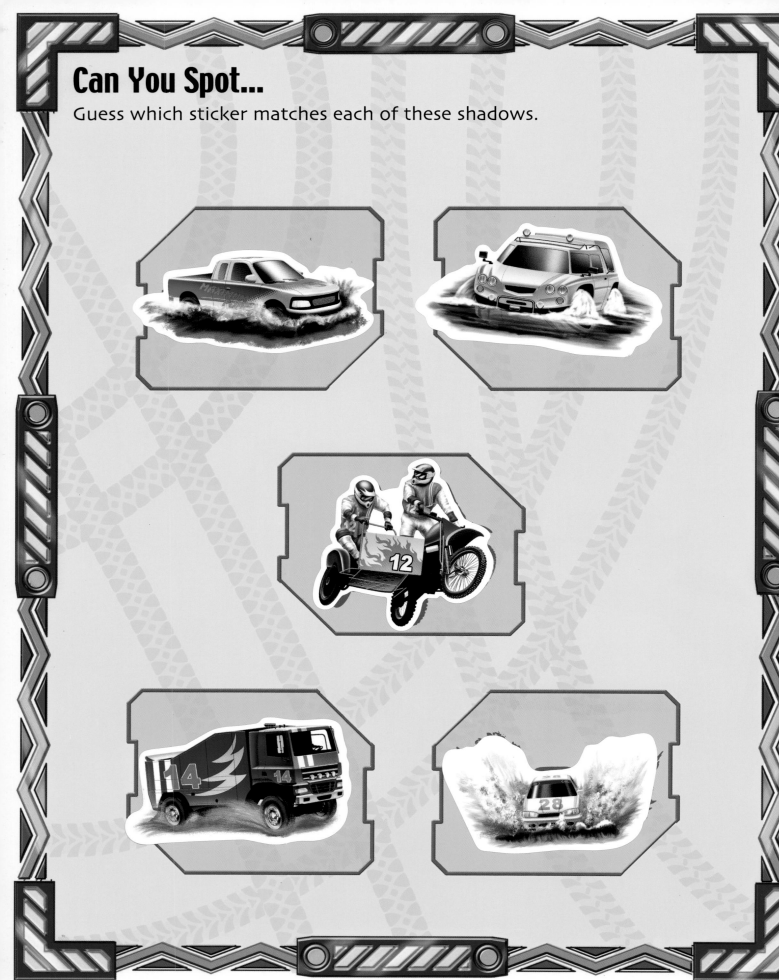

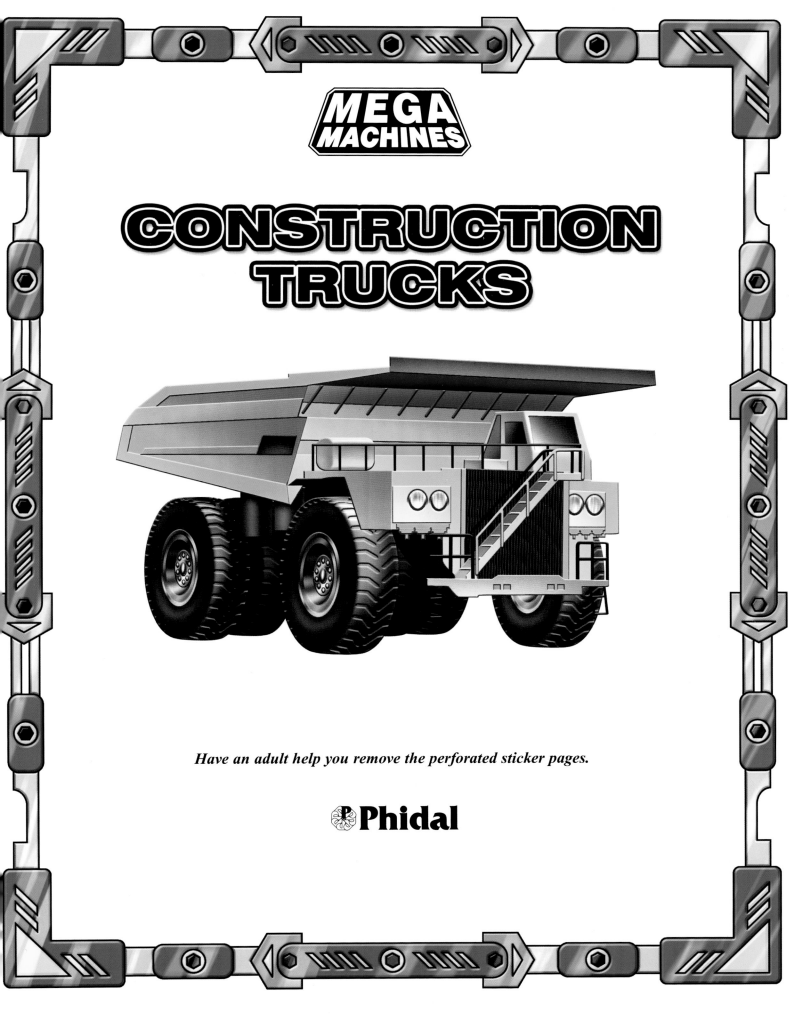

CONSTRUCTION TRUCKS

Have an adult help you remove the perforated sticker pages.

Phidal

Construction Facts

On a busy building site, all of the big construction machines have important jobs. They carry heavy materials and demolish old buildings.

Cranes lift heavy materials to the tops of tall buildings.

Dump trucks have double sets of tires to help support the weight of their load.

A motor grader levels the ground before the road is paved.

The compactor hardens the ground as it presses soil, stones, and asphalt.

A concrete mixer rolls and mixes concrete.

Mobile crushers break large objects into small pieces.

Most bulldozers use crawler tracks for gripping loose dirt and climbing rocky ground.

A wheel loader carries mud and loads it onto dump trucks.

Articulated dump trucks are great for getting around sharp curves on winding roads.

A hydraulic excavator digs the foundation for a new house.

Asphalt finishers spread asphalt over the road to make it more durable.

Did You Know That?

Without construction equipment, we wouldn't have tall skyscrapers, schools, or shopping malls. Place your stickers over the shadows.

Some trucks use crawlers to travel across uneven roads or difficult terrain.

This giant bulldozer measures over 10 yards long!

In dangerous areas, some equipment can be operated by remote control.

Each tire on a giant dump truck is as heavy as four station wagons!

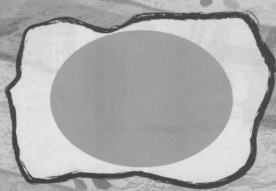

Tower cranes can rise and stretch out hundreds of feet into the air.

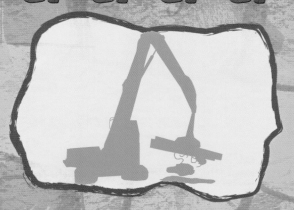

A lifting magnet attracts and separates metal from cement.

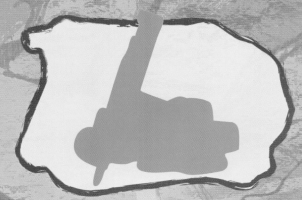

A drifter drill can dig holes up to 20 feet deep.

A concrete pulverizer breaks up concrete slabs with its huge jaw-like teeth.

A forklift truck can pile and stack heavy loads of bricks.

A backhoe loader digs from the back and shovels at the front.

A telescopic handler has an arm that reaches up to 48 feet in the air.

Building Zone

This construction team can expertly build homes. Bring the scene to life by adding your stickers to these building sites.

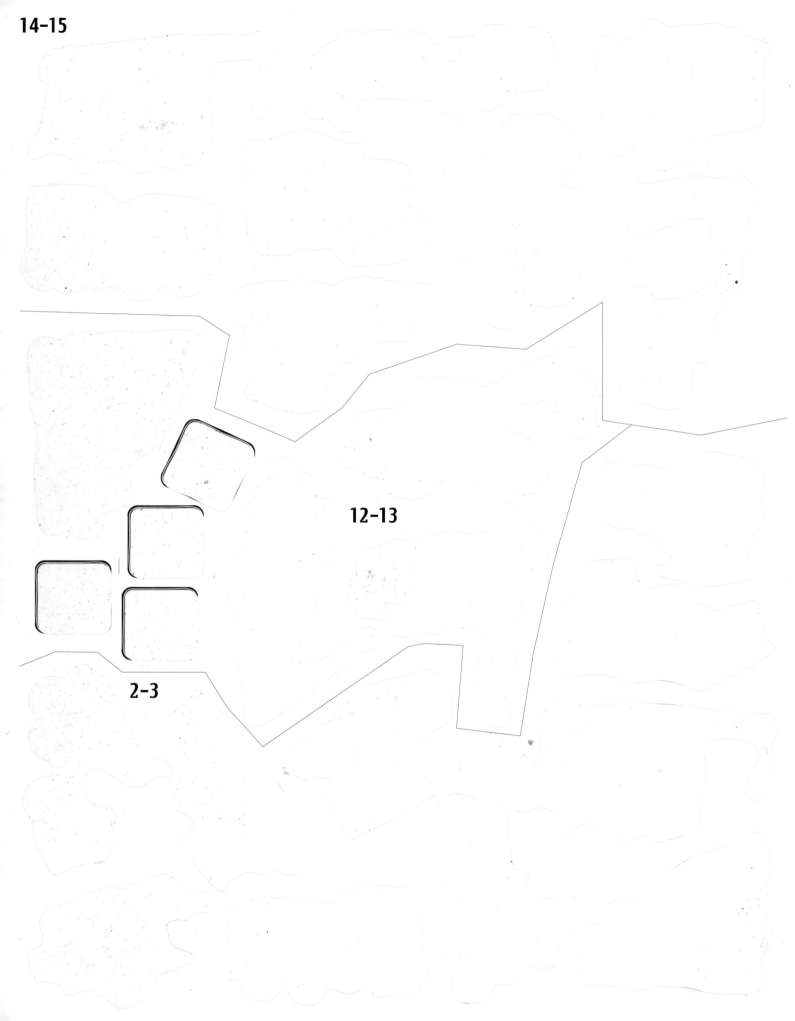

12–13

2–3

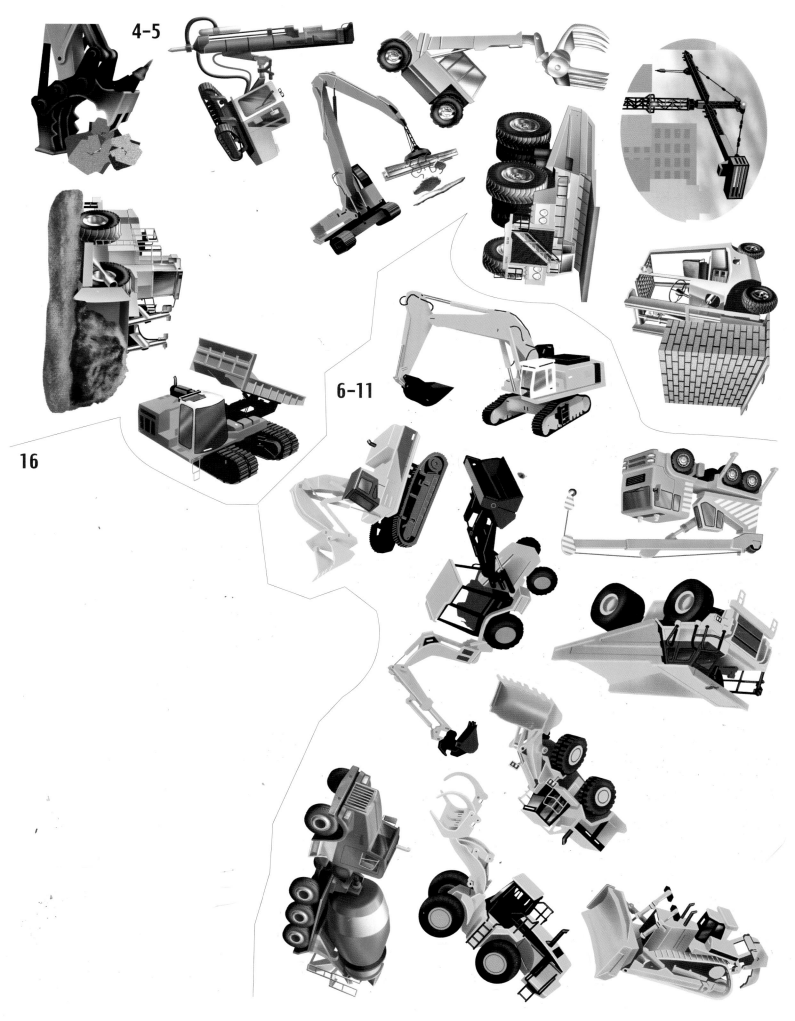

4-5

6-11

16

Matching Movements

Construction equipment often mimics human movements. Use your stickers to match the construction signs with the machines that perform the same job.

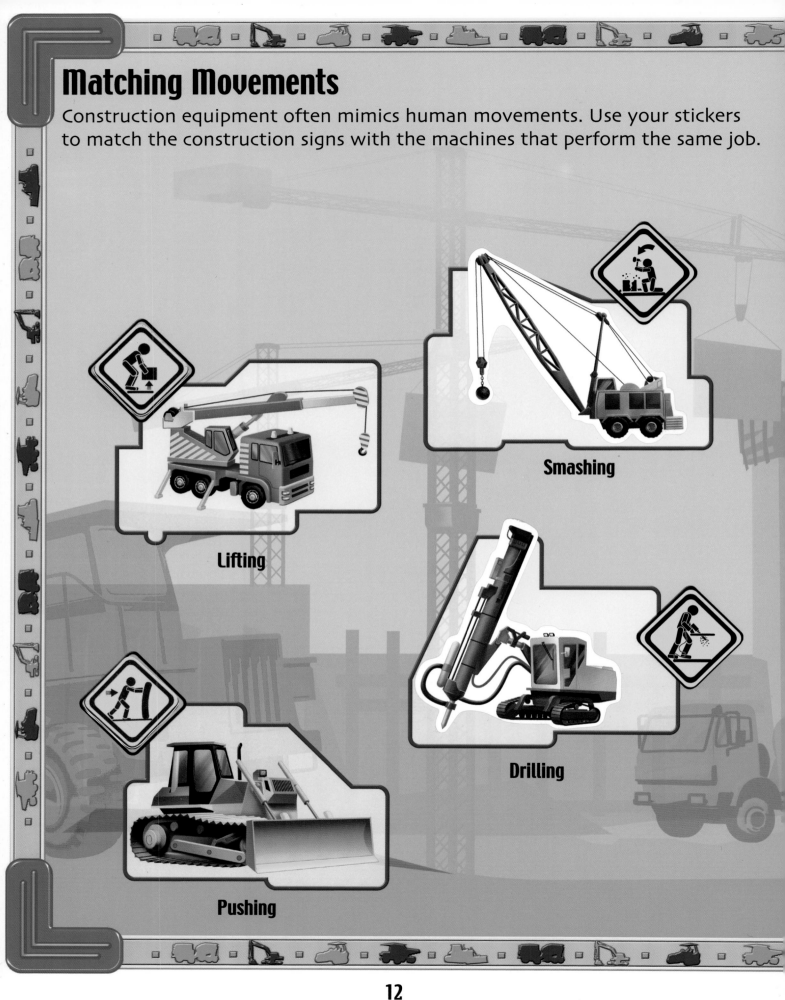

Smashing

Lifting

Drilling

Pushing

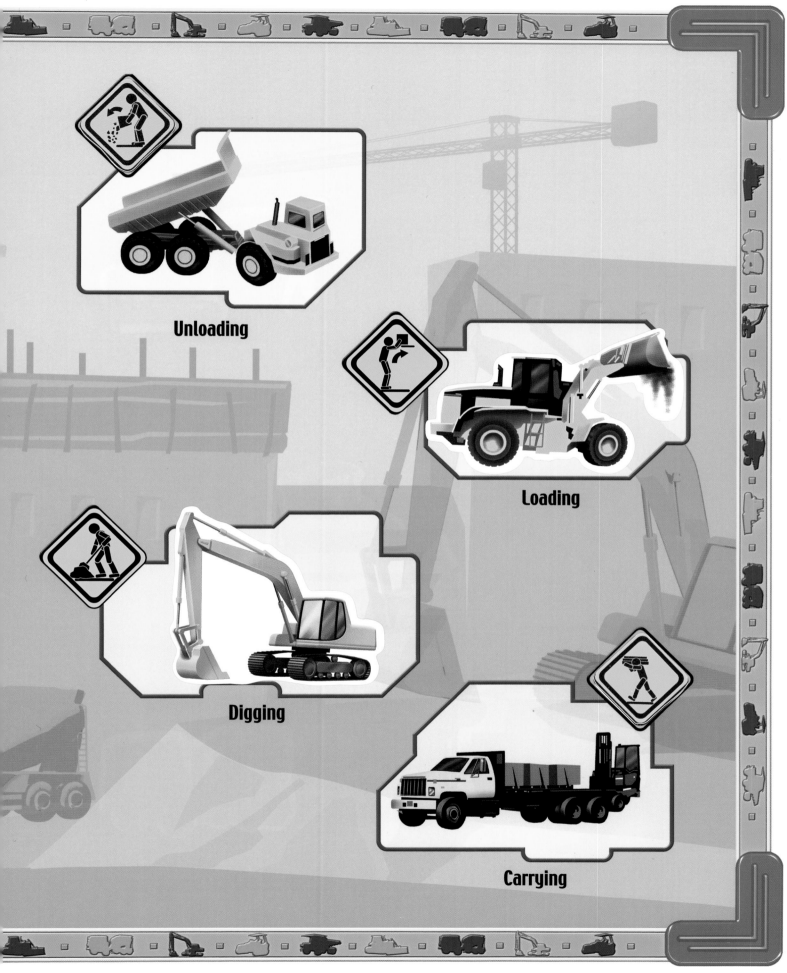

Unloading

Loading

Digging

Carrying

Ready, Set, Build!

Building a house is a big job, and every machine is important in the process! Place your stickers and discover all the steps needed to construct a house.

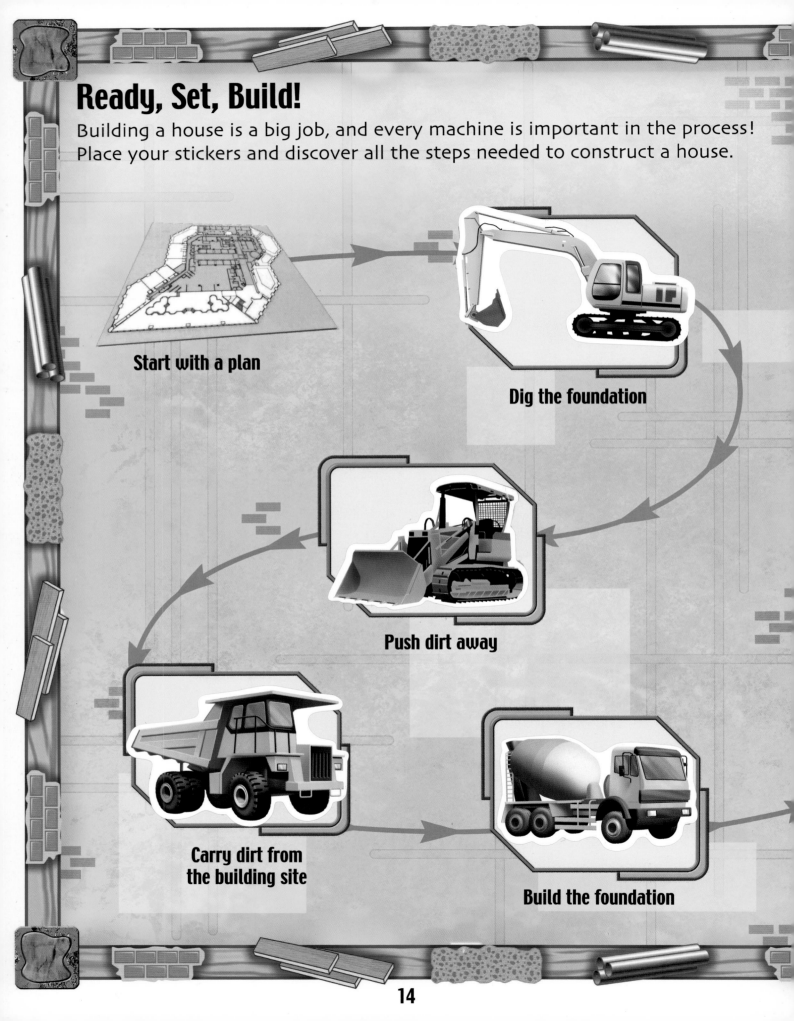

Start with a plan

Dig the foundation

Push dirt away

Carry dirt from the building site

Build the foundation

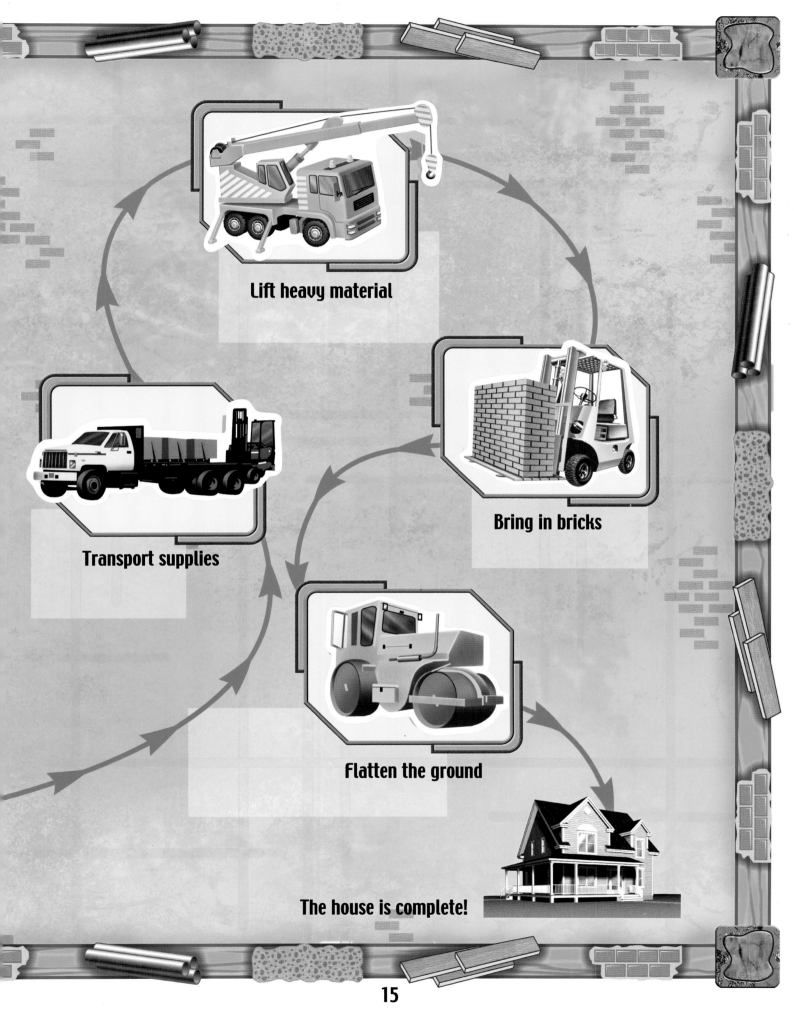

Lift heavy material

Bring in bricks

Transport supplies

Flatten the ground

The house is complete!

Can You Spot...

Guess which sticker matches each of these shadows.

MEGA MACHINES

HELICOPTERS

Have an adult help you remove the perforated sticker pages.

Phidal

Helicopter Facts

Helicopters are the most versatile flying machines in the world. Piloting one requires intense training and skill.

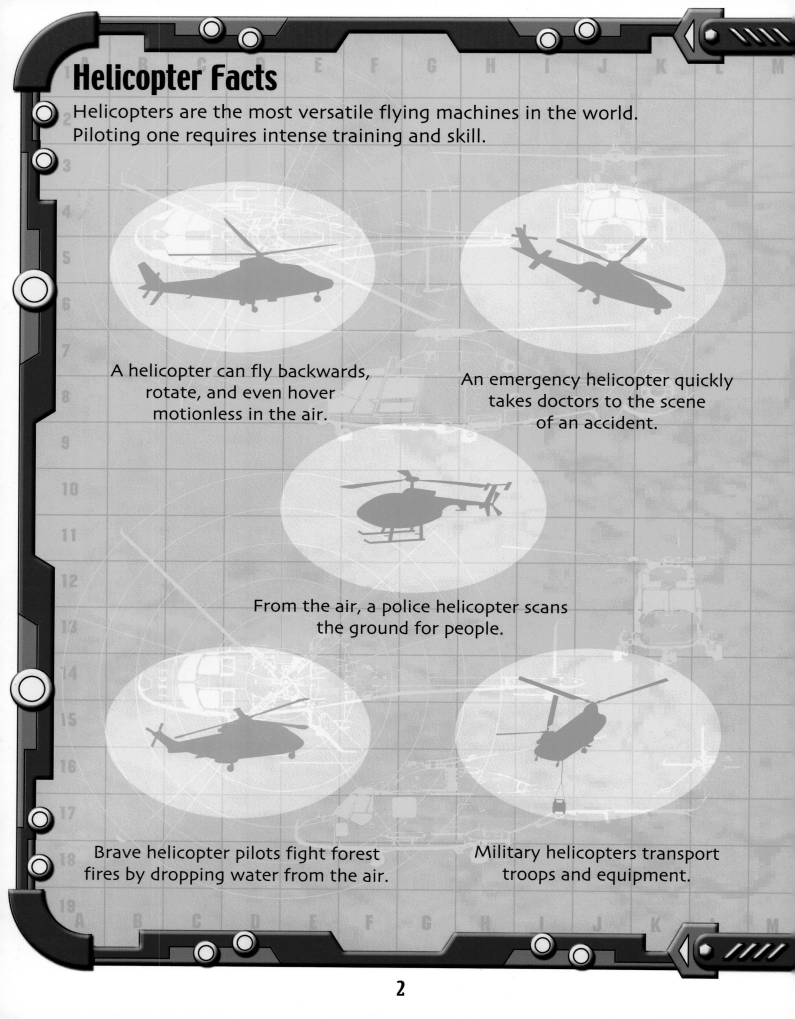

A helicopter can fly backwards, rotate, and even hover motionless in the air.

An emergency helicopter quickly takes doctors to the scene of an accident.

From the air, a police helicopter scans the ground for people.

Brave helicopter pilots fight forest fires by dropping water from the air.

Military helicopters transport troops and equipment.

Helicopter pilots can work in law enforcement, agriculture, and emergency services.

Construction helicopters are strong enough to carry heavy cargo through the air.

A rescue helicopter uses a long cable to lift people out of dangerous situations.

Some helicopters are operated by remote control in areas too dangerous for humans.

Some helicopters can actually land on water instead of solid ground!

Controllers direct helicopters from the control tower.

Did You Know That?

Helicopters can take off and land vertically, which helps make them the most maneuverable of all aircraft.

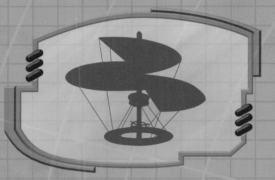

Leonardo da Vinci was the first to create sketches of the helicopter over 500 years ago.

Rotator blades act like huge propellers and pull helicopters up in the air.

 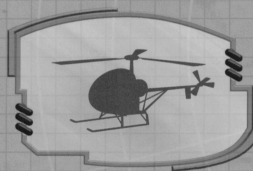

Without tail rotators for balance, helicopters would spin out of control!

Small helicopters can be used for personal flight or business.

Air paramedics are equipped with rescue harnesses to lower themselves to the scene.

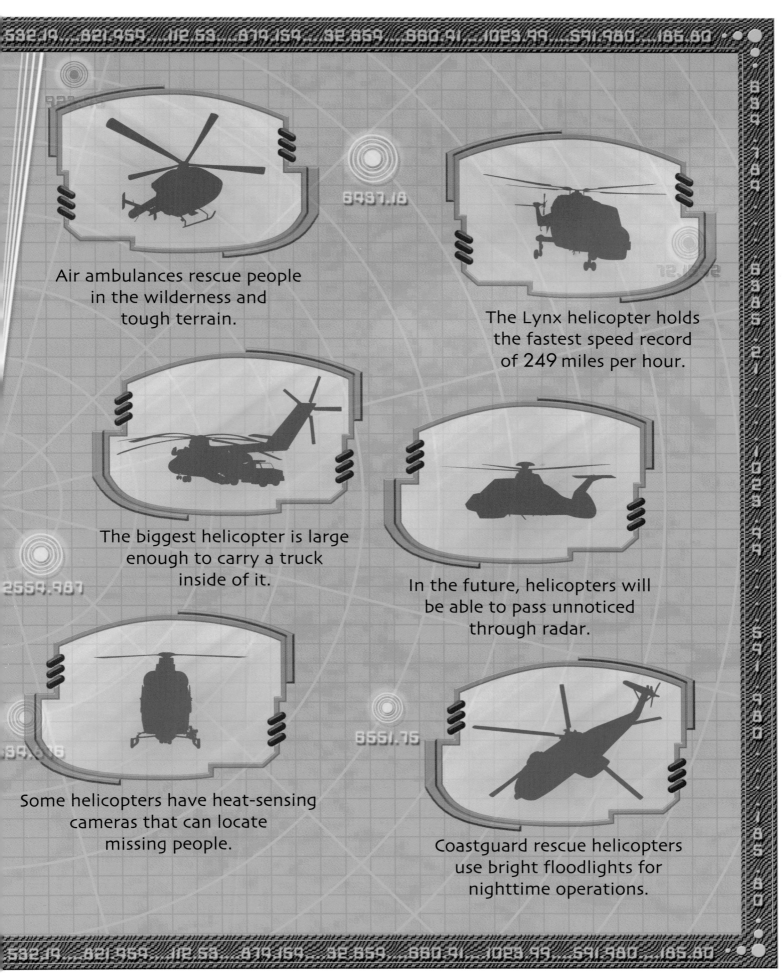

Air ambulances rescue people in the wilderness and tough terrain.

The Lynx helicopter holds the fastest speed record of 249 miles per hour.

The biggest helicopter is large enough to carry a truck inside of it.

In the future, helicopters will be able to pass unnoticed through radar.

Some helicopters have heat-sensing cameras that can locate missing people.

Coastguard rescue helicopters use bright floodlights for nighttime operations.

On the Job

A fleet of helicopters is patrolling the skies. Use your stickers to create air traffic over this scene.

12–13

4–5

14–15

16

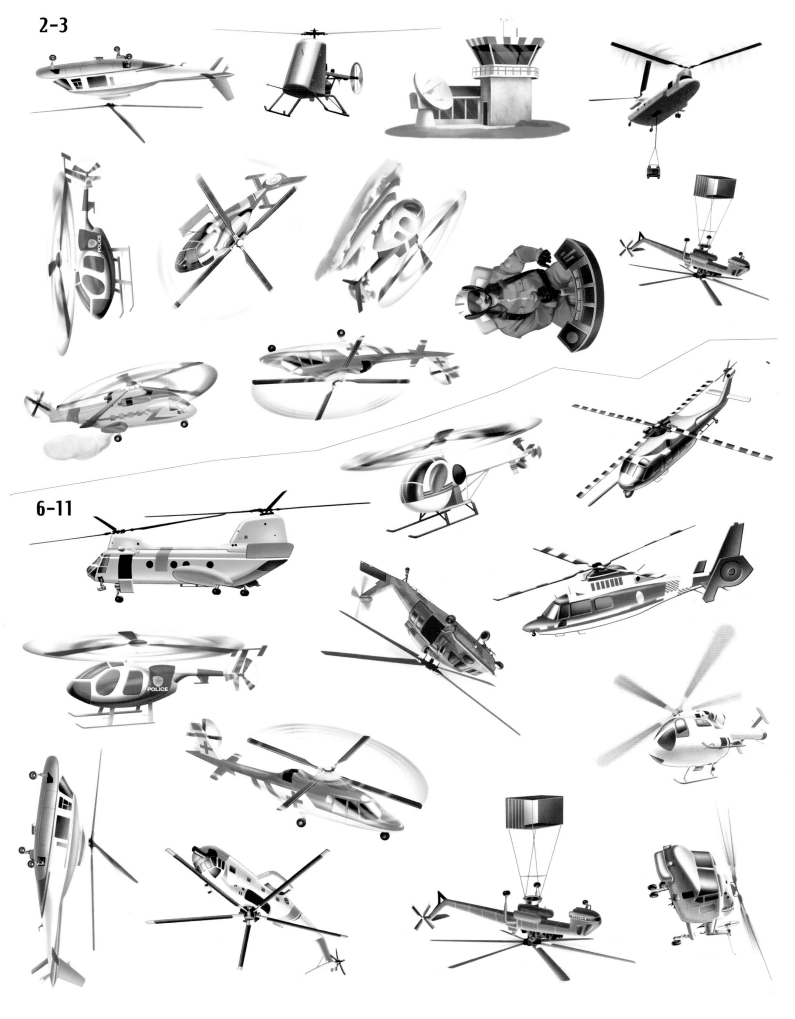

2-3

6-11

Major Match-Up

Now that you've learned about the different jobs helicopters can perform, place each one beside the equipment or scene it matches.

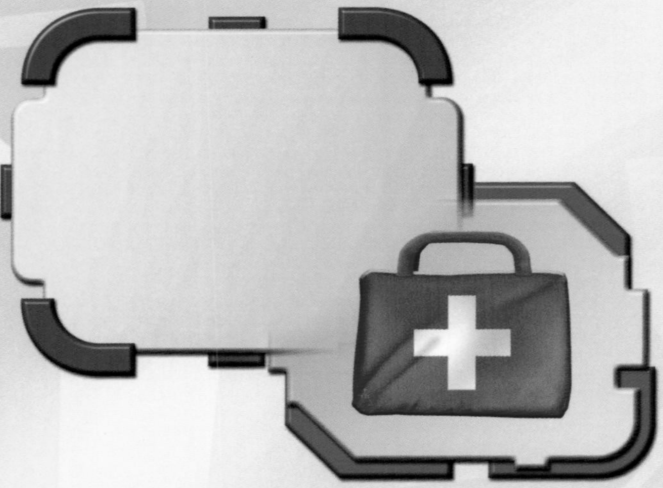

Air ambulance

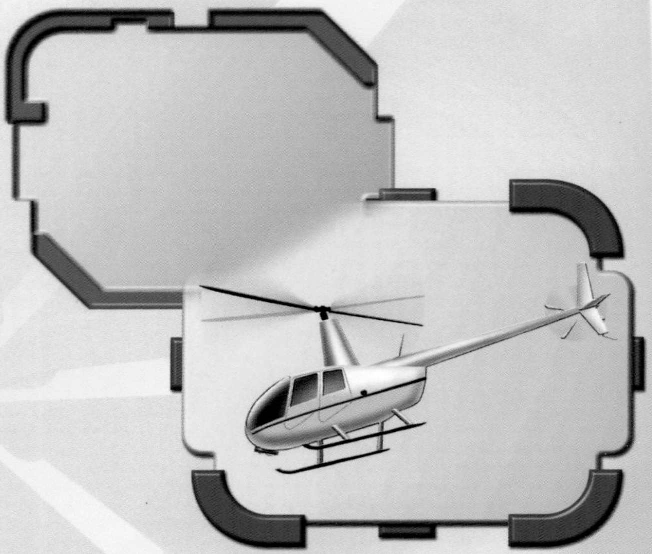

Camera helicopter

Construction helicopter

Military helicopter

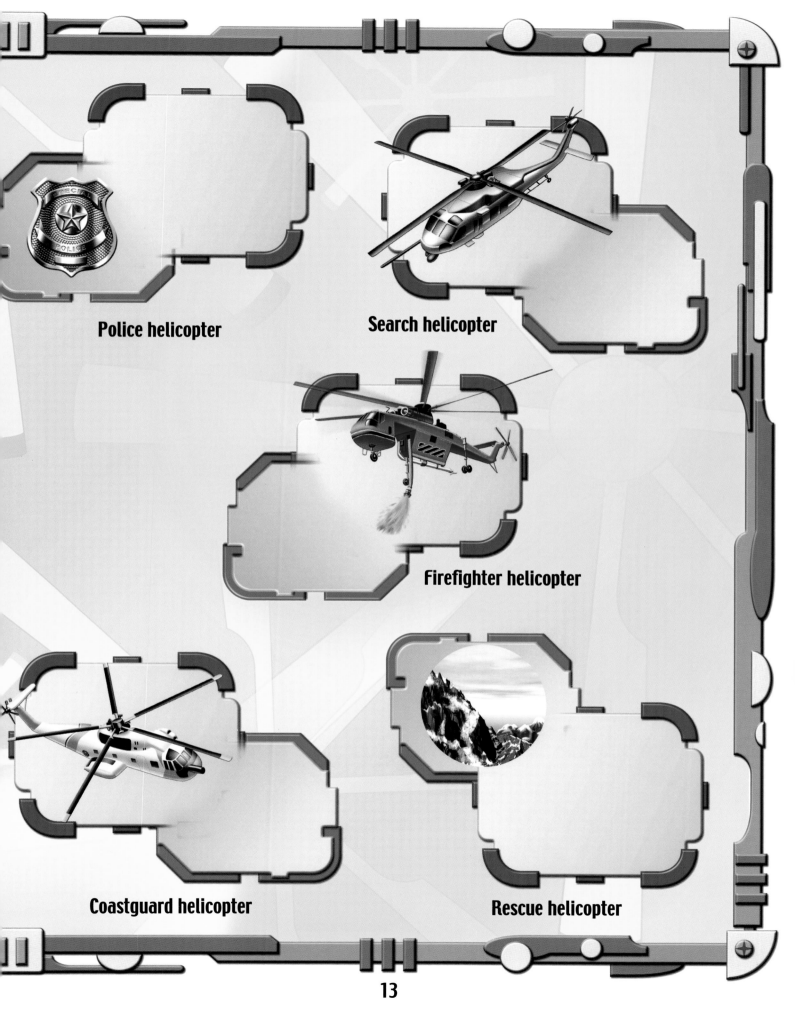

Police helicopter

Search helicopter

Firefighter helicopter

Coastguard helicopter

Rescue helicopter

Mission Accomplished

Helicopters are used in dangerous rescues and military missions. Use your stickers to discover what each helicopter needs to complete the mission.

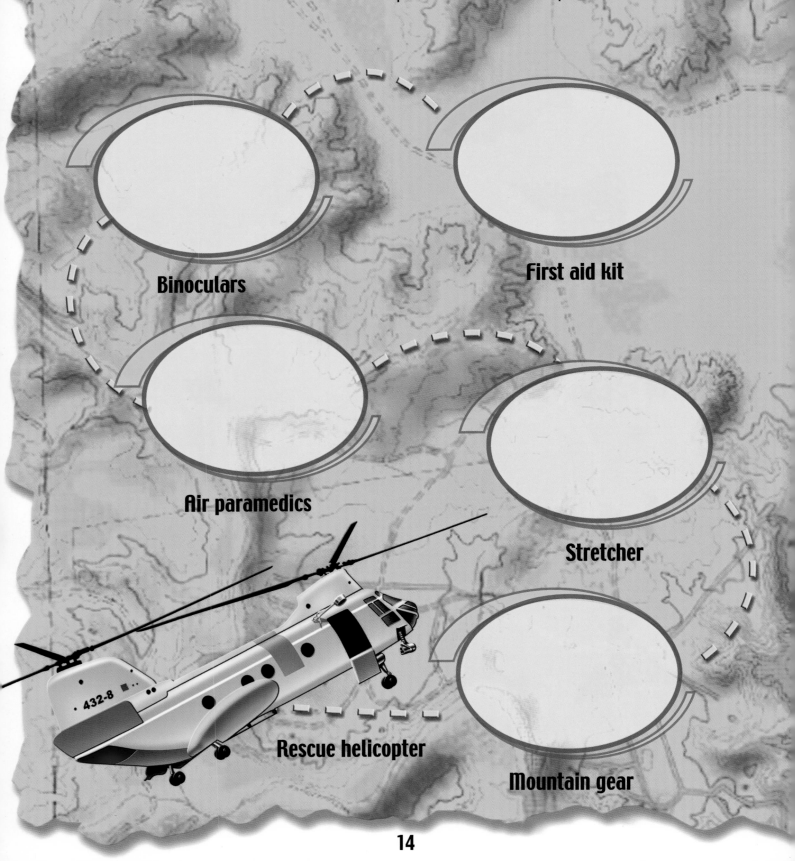

Binoculars

First aid kit

Air paramedics

Stretcher

Rescue helicopter

Mountain gear

432-8

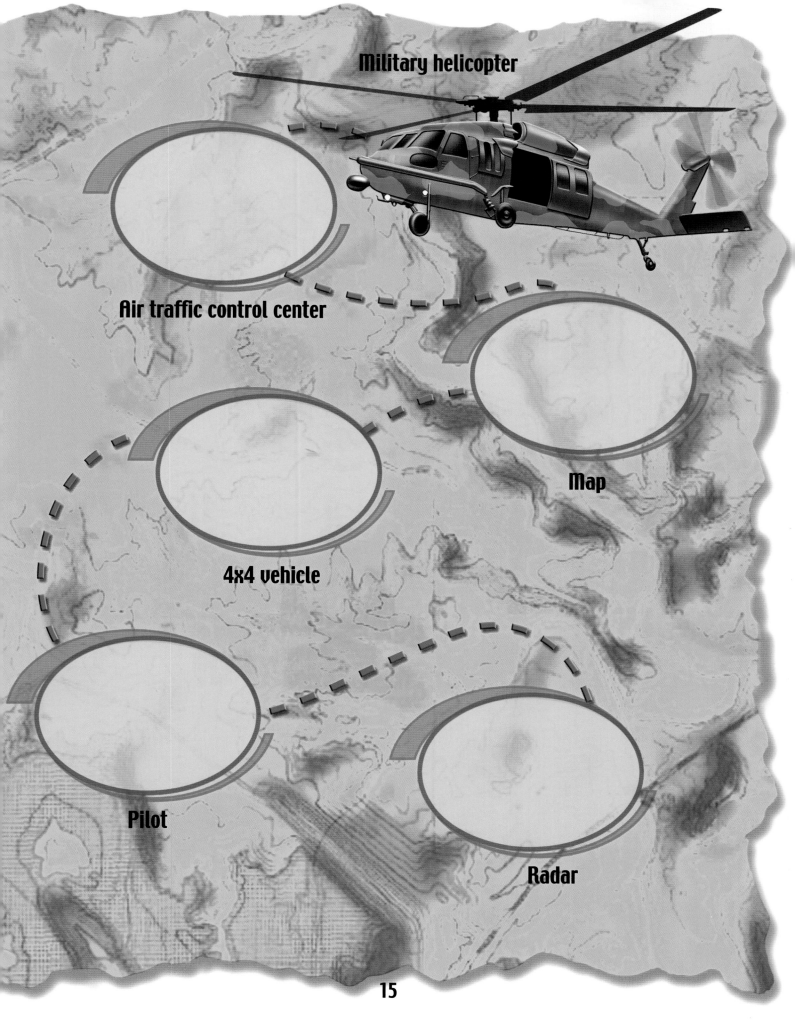

Military helicopter

Air traffic control center

Map

4x4 vehicle

Pilot

Radar

15

Can You Spot...

Guess which sticker matches each of these shadows.

TRAINS

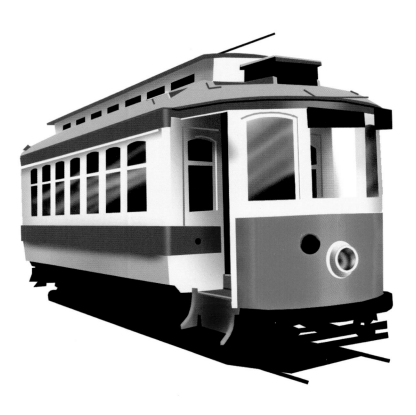

Have an adult help you remove the perforated sticker pages.

Train Facts

It's hard to imagine what life would be like without trains. They help carry people and supplies through busy cities and to remote regions.

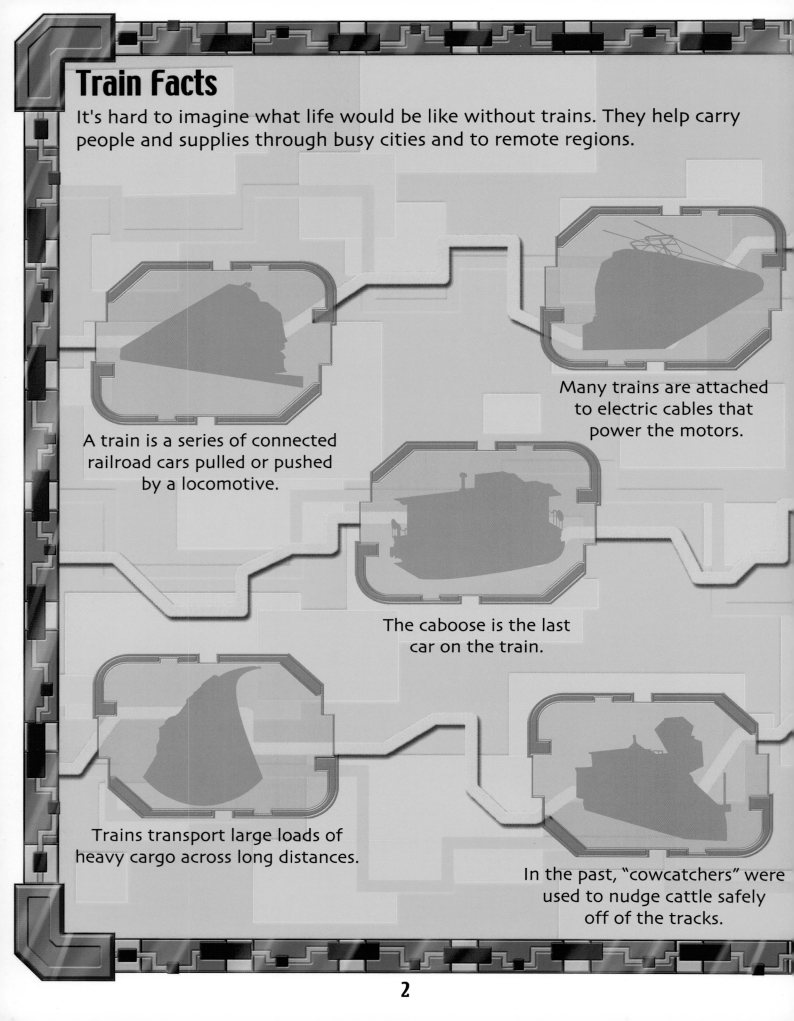

A train is a series of connected railroad cars pulled or pushed by a locomotive.

Many trains are attached to electric cables that power the motors.

The caboose is the last car on the train.

Trains transport large loads of heavy cargo across long distances.

In the past, "cowcatchers" were used to nudge cattle safely off of the tracks.

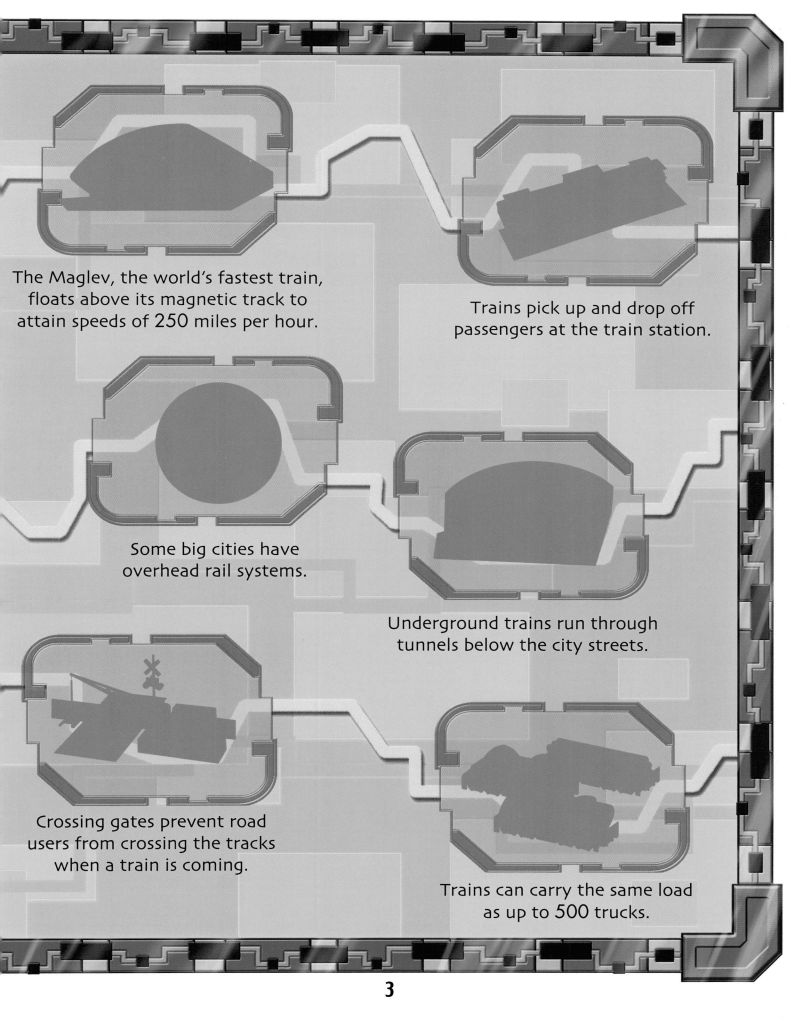

The Maglev, the world's fastest train, floats above its magnetic track to attain speeds of 250 miles per hour.

Trains pick up and drop off passengers at the train station.

Some big cities have overhead rail systems.

Underground trains run through tunnels below the city streets.

Crossing gates prevent road users from crossing the tracks when a train is coming.

Trains can carry the same load as up to 500 trucks.

Did You Know That?

The first railroad networks appeared in Britain in the 1800s, and are found all over the world today. Use your stickers to find out more.

The first locomotives ran on steam produced by coal-burning fires.

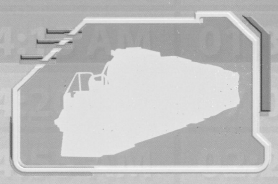

The largest steam locomotives, known as "Big Boys", weighed more than 1.2 million pounds!

A Japanese railway carries the most passengers in the world, over 16 million every day!

Freight containers can be transferred from trains onto boats.

A bullet train can travel very fast because its tracks have no sharp curves.

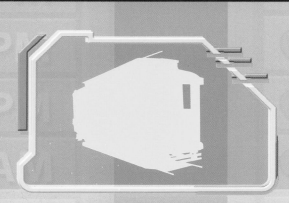

San Francisco is famous for traditional cable cars, which can handle the steep city streets.

Tampers maintain railroad safety by keeping the railway tracks straight and flat.

Some trains can remove snow from the track with sturdy plow cars.

The circus was the talk of the town when its ornate train cars pulled into the station.

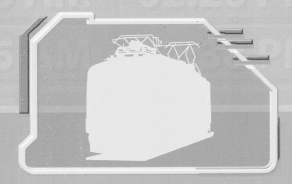

Passengers can travel for more than six days across Russia on the Trans-Siberian Railway.

The world's longest train is over 4 miles long - that's more than 700 school buses!

All Aboard!

Model trains are great to collect and a blast to assemble! Put together this train set by arranging your stickers on the page.

16

4–5

12–13

6–11

2-3

14-15

6-11

What's Missing?

Trains carry every kind of cargo across countries and continents. Use your stickers to fill up the train cars.

Can You Spot...
Guess which sticker matches each of these shadows.

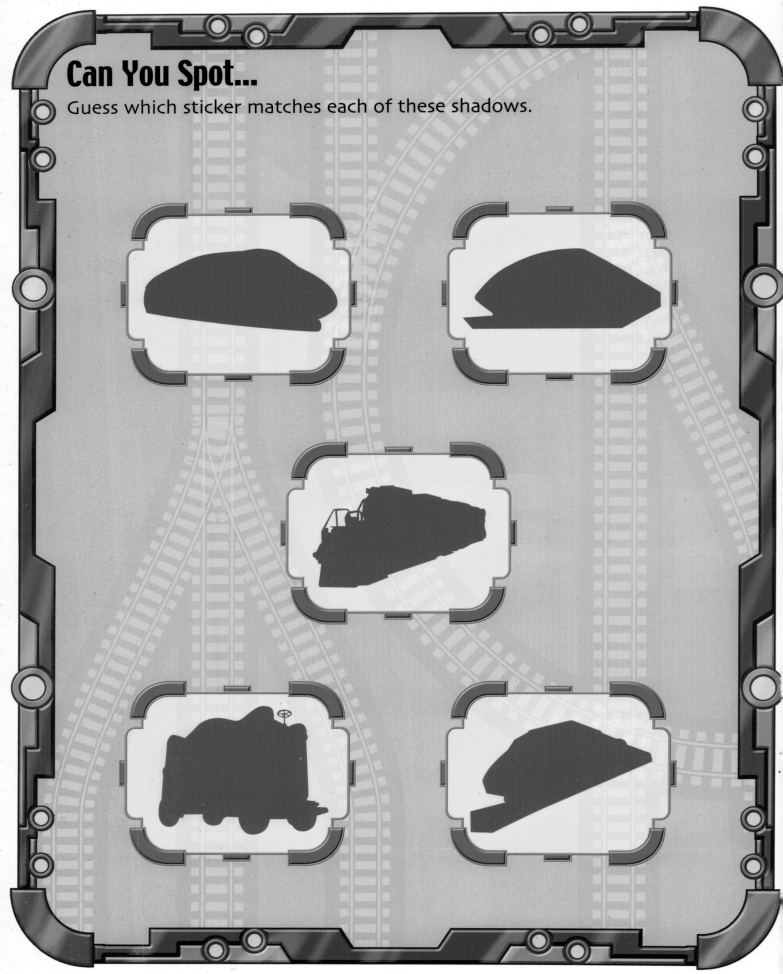